A Moment Here

At first, bewilders us the light's surprise,
As blinkingly, its filtered to our eyes,
From where we came, or whence or why we go,
It never was intended we should know.

While yet we coo, the days of Life decline.
Then, shall we live, as did Evangeline?
Should, you be disconsolate, arise
And watch the mounting Sun in Eastern skies.

For Venus sows her seed in barren clays,
If thirst you quench with dreams of other days.
On dried up sand will die the desert bloom.
Destruction rides a chariot of gloom.

Live as though tomorrow were today,
Art sure, the Cock again will crow and say,
"The day begins, arise and sing your best,
For soon the Sun will darken in the West"?

The dust of Souls around you blows,
This or that, a speck of whom — who knows?
Ah, whom every speck would cause to hesitate,
Must hear a warning trumpet from Old Fate.

Hasten, child of soil, ahead is dust,
In whose dominion you in time shall trust.
From, just a moment here, a moment there,
Soon you'll be the swirling dust of everywhere.

J. Howard Snively
1940

RUBÁIYÁT · OF
OMAR · KHAYYÁM

Merry Xmas, Dec 1940
To Cleda
from Papa Snively.

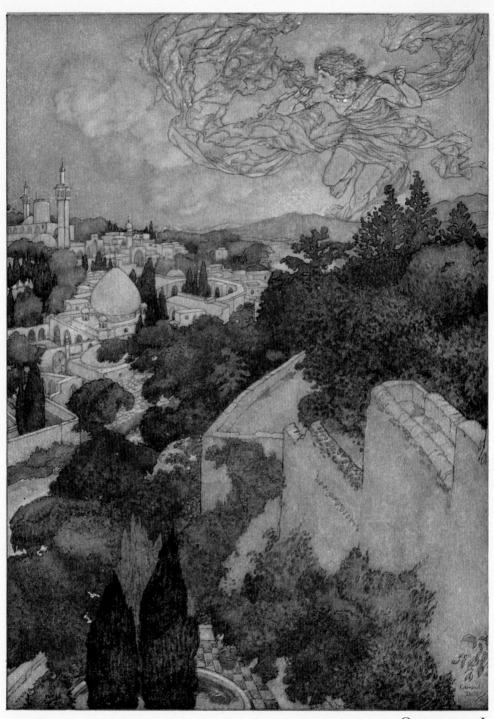

QUATRAIN I

RUBÁIYÁT
OF
OMAR
KHAYYÁM

RENDERED INTO ENGLISH VERSE BY
Edward Fitzgerald

WITH ILLUSTRATIONS BY
Edmund Dulac

DE LUXE EDITION
GARDEN CITY PUBLISHING CO., INC.
New York

1937

GARDEN CITY PUBLISHING CO., INC.

CL

CONTENTS AND ILLUSTRATIONS

BIOGRAPHICAL PREFACE

EDWARD FITZGERALD

EDWARD FITZGERALD, whom the world has already learned, in spite of his own efforts to remain within the shadow of anonymity, to look upon as one of the rarest poets of the last century, was born at Bredfield, in Suffolk, on the 31st March, 1809. He was the third son of John Purcell, of Kilkenny, in Ireland, who, marrying Miss Mary Frances Fitzgerald, daughter of John Fitzgerald, of Williamstown, County Waterford, added that distinguished name to his own patronymic; and the future Omar was thus doubly of Irish extraction. (Both the families of Purcell and Fitzgerald claim descent from Norman warriors of the eleventh century.) This circumstance is thought to have had some influence in attracting him to the study of Persian poetry, Iran and Erin being almost convertible terms in the early days of modern ethnology. After some years of primary education at the grammar school of Bury St. Edmunds, he entered Trinity College, Cambridge, in 1826, and there formed acquaintance with several young men of great abilities, most of whom rose to distinction before him, but never ceased to regard with affectionate remembrance the quiet and amiable associate of their college-days. Amongst them were Alfred Tennyson, James Spedding, William Bod-

ham Donne, John Mitchell Kemble, and William
Makepeace Thackeray; and their long friendship
was touchingly referred to by Tennyson in dedi-
cating his last poem to the memory of Edward
Fitzgerald. "Euphranor," our author's earliest
printed work, affords a curious picture of his
academic life and associations. Its substantial real-
ity is evident beneath the thin disguise of the sym-
bolical or classical names which he gives to the per-
sonages of the colloquy; and the speeches which he
puts into his own mouth are full of the humorous
gravity, and whimsical and kindly philosophy,
which remained his distinguishing characteristics
till the end. This book was first published in 1851;
a second and a third edition were printed some
years later; all anonymous, and each of the latter
two differing from its predecessor by changes in
the text which were not indicated on the title-
pages.

"Euphranor" furnishes a good many characteri-
zations which would be useful for any writer treat-
ing upon Cambridge society in the third decade of
this century. Kenelm Digby, the author of the
"Broadstone of Honour," had left Cambridge before the time when Euphranor held his "dialogue,"
but he is picturesquely recollected as "a grand
swarthy fellow who might have stepped out of the
canvas of some knightly portrait in his father's
hall—perhaps the living image of one sleeping under some cross-legged *effigies* in the church." In
"Euphranor," it is easy to discover the earliest phase
of the unconquerable attachment which Fitzgerald
entertained for his college and his life-long friends,

and which induced him in later days to make frequent visits to Cambridge, renewing and refreshing the old ties of custom and friendship. In fact, his disposition was affectionate to a fault, and he betrayed his consciousness of weakness in that respect by referring playfully at times to "a certain natural lubricity" which he attributed to the Irish character, and professed to discover especially in himself. This amiability of temper endeared him to many friends of totally dissimilar tastes and qualities; and, by enlarging his sympathies, enabled him to enjoy the fructifying influence of studies pursued in communion with scholars more profound than himself, but less gifted with the power of expression. One of the younger Cambridge men with whom he became intimate during his periodical pilgrimages to the university, was Edward B. Cowell, a man of the highest attainment in Oriental learning, who resembled Fitzgerald himself in the possession of a warm and genial heart and the most unobtrusive modesty. From Cowell he could easily learn that the hypothetical affinity between the names of Erin and Iran belonged to an obsolete stage of etymology; but the attraction of a far-fetched theory was replaced by the charm of reading Persian poetry in companionship with his young friend, who was equally competent to enjoy and to analyze the beauties of a literature that formed a portion of his regular studies. They read together the poetical remains of Khayyám—a choice of reading which sufficiently indicates the depth and range of Mr. Cowell's knowledge. Omar Khayyám, although not quite forgotten, en-

joyed in the history of Persian literature a celebrity
like that of Occleve and Gower in our own. In the
many *Tazkirát* (memoirs or memorials) of Poets,
he was mentioned and quoted with esteem; but his
poems, laboring as they did under the original sin of
heresy and atheism, were seldom looked at, and, from
lack of demand on the part of readers, had become
rarer than those of most other writers since the days
of Firdausi. European scholars knew little of his
works beyond his Arabic treatise on Algebra, and
Mr. Cowell may be said to have disentombed his
poems from oblivion. Now, thanks to the fine
taste of that scholar, and to the transmuting genius
of Fitzgerald, no Persian poet is so well known in
the western world as Abu-'l-fat'h 'Omar, son of
Ibrahim the tentmaker of Naishápúr, whose man-
hood synchronizes with the Norman conquest of
England, and who took for his poetic name (*takhallus*) the designation of his father's trade
(*Khayyám*). The "Rubá'iyyát" (Quatrains) do
not compose a single poem divided into a certain
number of stanzas; there is no continuity of plan
in them, and each stanza is a distinct thought ex-
pressed in musical verse. There is no other element
of unity in them than the general tendency of the
Epicurean idea, and the arbitrary divan form by
which they are grouped according to the alphabetical arrangement of the final letters; those in
which the rhymes end in *a* constituting the first
division, those with *b* the second, and so on. The
peculiar attitude towards religion and the old questions of fate, immortality, the origin and the
destiny of man, which educated thinkers have as-

sumed in the present age of Christendom, is found admirably foreshadowed in the fantastic verses of Khayyám, who was no more of a Mohammedan than many of our best writers are Christians. His philosophical and Horatian fancies—graced as they are by the charms of a lyrical expression equal to that of Horace, and a vivid brilliance of imagination to which the Roman poet could make no claim—exercised a powerful influence upon Fitzgerald's mind, and colored his thoughts to such a degree that even when he oversteps the largest license allowed to a translator, his phrases reproduce the spirit and manner of his original with a nearer approach to perfection than would appear possible. It is usually supposed that there is more of Fitzgerald than of Khayyám in the English "Rubá'iyyát," and that the old Persian simply afforded themes for the Anglo-Irishman's display of poetic power; but nothing could be further from the truth. The French translator, J. B. Nicolas, and the English one, Mr. Whinfield, supply a closer mechanical reflection of the sense in each separate stanza; but Mr. Fitzgerald has, in some instances, given a version equally close and exact; in others, rejointed scattered phrases from more than one stanza of his original, and thus accomplished a feat of marvelous poetical transfusion. He frequently turns literally into English the strange outlandish imagery which Mr. Whinfield thought necessary to replace by more intelligible banalities, and in this way the magic of his genius has successfully transplanted into the garden of English poesy exotics that bloom like native flowers.

One of Mr. Fitzgerald's Woodbridge friends was
Bernard Barton, the Quaker poet, with whom he
maintained for many years the most intimate and
cordial intercourse, and whose daughter Lucy he
married. He wrote the memoir of his friend's life
which appeared in the posthumous volume of
Barton's poems. The story of his married life was
a short one. With all the overflowing amiability
of his nature, there were mingled certain peculiar-
ities or waywardnesses which were more suitable
to the freedom of celibacy than to the staidness of
matrimonial life. A separation took place by
mutual agreement, and Fitzgerald behaved in this
circumstance with the generosity and unselfishness
which were apparent in all his whims no less than
in his more deliberate actions. Indeed, his entire
career was marked by an unchanging goodness of
heart and a genial kindliness; and no one could
complain of having ever endured hurt or ill-treat-
ment at his hands. His pleasures were innocent
and simple. Amongst the more delightful, he
counted the short coasting trips, occupying no
more than a day or two at a time, which he used
to make in his own yacht from Lowestoft, accom-
panied only by a crew of two men, and such a
friend as Cowell, with a large pasty and a few
bottles of wine to supply their material wants. It
is needless to say that books were also put into the
cabin, and that the symposia of the friends were
thus brightened by communion with the minds of
the great departed. Fitzgerald's enjoyment of
gnomic wisdom enshrined in words of exquisite
propriety was evinced by the frequency with

which he used to read Montaigne's essays and Madame de Sévigné's letters, and the various works from which he extracted and published his collection of wise saws entitled "Polonius." This taste was allied to a love for what was classical and correct in literature, by which he was also enabled to appreciate the prim and formal muse of Crabbe, in whose grandson's house he died.

His second printed work was the "Polonius," already referred to, which appeared in 1852. It exemplifies his favorite reading, being a collection of extracts, sometimes short proverbial phrases, sometimes longer pieces of characterization or reflection, arranged under abstract headings. He occasionally quotes Dr. Johnson, for whom he entertains sincere admiration; but the ponderous and artificial fabric of Johnsonese did not please him like the language of Bacon, Fuller, Sir Thomas Browne, Coleridge, whom he cites frequently. A disproportionate abundance of wise words was drawn from Carlyle; his original views, his forcible sense, and the friendship with which Fitzgerald regarded him, having apparently blinded the latter to the ungainly style and ungraceful mannerisms of the Chelsea sage. (It was Thackeray who first made them personally acquainted; and Fitzgerald remained always loyal to his first instincts of affection and admiration.) Polonius also marks the period of his earliest attention to Persian studies, as he quotes in it the great Sufi poet, Jalál-ud-dín-Rúmi, whose "Masnavi" has been translated into English by Mr. Redhouse, but whom Fitzgerald can only have seen in the original. He, however.

spells the name *Jallaladin,* an incorrect form of
which he could not have been guilty at the time
when he produced Omar Khayyám, and which
thus betrays that he had not long been engaged
with Irani literature. He was very fond of Montaigne's essays, and of Pascal's "Pensées"; but his
"Polonius" reveals a sort of dislike and contempt
for Voltaire. Amongst the Germans, Jean Paul,
Goethe, Alexander von Humboldt and August
Wilhelm von Schegel attracted him greatly; but
he seems to have read little German, and probably
only quoted translations. His favorite motto was
"Plain Living and High Thinking," and he ex-
presses great reverence for all things manly, simple,
and true. The laws and institutions of England
were, in his eyes, of the highest value and sacred-
ness; and whatever Irish sympathies he had would
never have diverted his affections from the Union
to Home Rule. This is strongly illustrated by
some original lines of blank verse at the end of
"Polonius," annexed to his quotation, under "Æs-
thetics," of the words in which Lord Palmerston
eulogized Mr. Gladstone for having devoted his
Neapolitan tour to an inspection of the prisons.

Fitzgerald's next printed work was a translation
of Six Dramas of Calderon, published in 1853,
which was unfavorably received at the time, and
consequently withdrawn by him from circulation.
His name appeared on the title-page,—a concession
to publicity which was so unusual with him that
it must have been made under strong pressure from
his friends. The book is in nervous blank verse, a
mode of composition which he handled with great

ease and skill. There is no waste of power in diffuseness and no employment of unnecessary epithets. It gives the impression of a work of the Shakespearean age, and reveals a kindred felicity, strength, and directness of language. It deserves to rank with his best efforts in poetry, but its ill-success made him feel that the publication of his name was an unfavorable experiment, and he never again repeated it. His great modesty, however, would sufficiently account for his shyness. Of "Omar Khayyám," even after the little book had won its way to general esteem, he used to say that the suggested addition of his name on the title would imply an assumption of importance which he considered that his "transmogrification" of the Persian poet did not possess.

Fitzgerald's conception of a translator's privilege is well set forth in the prefaces of his versions from Calderon, and the "Agamemnon" of Æschylus. He maintained that, in the absence of the perfect poet, who shall re-create in his own language the body and soul of his original, the best system is that of a paraphrase conserving the spirit of the author,—a sort of literary metempsychosis. Calderon, Æschylus, and Omar Khayyám were all treated with equal license, so far as form is concerned,—the last, perhaps, the most arbitrarily; but the result is not unsatisfactory as having given us perfect English poems instinct with the true flavor of their prototypes. The Persian was probably somewhat more Horatian and less melancholy, the Greek a little less florid and mystic, the Spaniard more lyrical and fluent, than their metaphrast has made them; but the essential spirit has not escaped in transfusion. Only a man of singular gifts could have perfomed the achievement, and these works attest Mr. Fitzgerald's right to rank amongst the finest poets of the century. About the same time as he printed his Calderon, another set of translations from the same dramatist was published by the late D. F. MacCarthy, a scholar whose acquaintance with Castilian literature was much deeper than Mr. Fitzgerald's, and who also possessed poetical abilities of no mean order, with a totally different sense of the translator's duty. The popularity of MacCarthy's versions has been considerable, and as an equivalent rendering of the original in sense and form his work is valuable. Spaniards familiar with the English language rate its merit highly; but there can be little question of the very great superiority of Mr. Fitzgerald's work as a contribution to English literature. It is indeed only from this point of view that we should regard all the literary labors of our author. They are English poetical work of fine quality, dashed with a pleasant outlandish flavor which heightens their charm; and it is as English poems, not as translations, that they have endeared themselves even more to the American English than to the mixed Britons of England.

It was an occasion of no small moment to Mr. Fitzgerald's fame, and to the intellectual gratification of many thousands of readers, when he took his little packet of "Rubá'iyyát" to Mr. Quaritch in the latter part of the year 1858. It was printed as a small quarto pamphlet, bearing the publisher's

name but not the author's; and although apparently
a complete failure at first,—a failure which Mr.
Fitzgerald regretted less on his own account than
on that of his publisher, to whom he had generously
made a present of the book,—received, neverthe-
less, a sufficient distribution by being quickly reduced from the price of five shillings and placed
in the box of cheap books marked a penny each.
Thus forced into circulation, the two hundred
copies which had been printed were soon exhausted.
Among the buyers were Dante Gabriel Rossetti,
Swinburne, Sir Richard Burton, and William
Simpson, the accomplished artist of the *Illustrated
London News*. The influence exercised by the first
three, especially by Rossetti, upon a clique of young
men who later grew to distinction, was sufficient
to attract observation to the singular beauties of
the poem anonymously translated from the Persian.
Most readers had no possible opportunity of dis-
covering whether it was a disguised original or an
actual translation;—even Burton enjoyed probably
but little chance of seeing a manuscript of the
Persian "Rubá'iyyát." The Oriental imagery and
allusions were too thickly scattered throughout
the verses to favor the notion that they could be
the original work of an Englishman; yet it was
shrewdly suspected by most of the appreciative
readers that the "translator" was substantially the
author and creator of the poem. In the refuge
of his anonymity, Fitzgerald derived an innocent
gratification from the curiosity that was aroused
on all sides. After the first edition had dis-
appeared, inquiries for the little book became fre-

quent, and in the year 1868 he gave the MS. of his second edition to Mr. Quaritch, and the "Rubá'-iyyát" came into circulation once more, but with several alterations and additions by which the number of stanzas was somewhat increased beyond the original seventy-five. Most of the changes were, as might have been expected, improvements; but in some instances the author's taste or caprice was at fault,—notably in the first *Rubá'iy*. His fastidious desire to avoid anything that seemed *baroque* or unnatural or appeared like plagiarism, may have influenced him; but it was probably because he had already used the idea in his rendering of Jámí's "Salámán," that he sacrificed a fine and novel piece of imagery in his first stanza and replaced it by one of much more ordinary character. If it were from a dislike to pervert his original too largely, he had no need to be so scrupulous, since he dealt on the whole with the "Rubá'iyyát" as though he had the license of absolute authorship, changing, transposing, and manipulating the substance of the Persian quatrains with a singular freedom. The vogue of "old Omar" (as he would affectionately call his work) went on increasing, and American readers took it up with eagerness. In those days the mere mention of Omar Khayyám between two strangers meeting fortuitously acted like a sign of freemasonry and established frequently a bond of friendship. Some curious instances of this have been related. A remarkable feature of the Omar-cult in the United States was the circumstance that single individuals bought numbers of copies for gratuitous distribution before the book was reprinted in America. Its editions have been relatively numerous, when we consider how restricted was the circle of readers who could understand the peculiar beauties of the work. A third edition appeared in 1872, with some further alterations, and may be regarded as virtually the author's final revision, for it hardly differs at all from the text of the fourth edition, which appeared in 1879. This last formed the first portion of a volume entitled "Rubáiyát of Omar Khayyám; and the Salámán and Absál of Jámí; rendered into English verse." The "Salámán" (which had already been printed in separate form in 1856) is a poem chiefly in blank verse, interspersed with various meters (although it is all in one measure in the original) embodying a love-story of mystic significance; for Jámí was, unlike Omar Khayyám, a true Súfi, and indeed differed in other respects, his celebrity as a pious Mussulman doctor being equal to his fame as a poet. He lived in the fifteenth century, in a period of literary brilliance and decay; and the rich exuberance of his poetry, full of far-fetched conceits, involved expressions, overstrained imagery, and false taste, offers a strong contrast to the simpler and more forcible language of Khayyám. There is little use of Arabic in the earlier poet; he preferred the vernacular speech to the mongrel language which was fashionable among the heirs of the Saracen conquerors; but Jámí's composition is largely embroidered with Arabic.

Mr. Fitzgerald had from his early days been thrown into contact with the Crabbe family; the

Reverend George Crabbe (the poet's grandson) was an intimate friend of his, and it was on a visit to Morton Rectory that Fitzgerald died. As we know that friendship has power to warp the judgment, we shall not probably be wrong in supposing that his enthusiastic admiration for Crabbe's poems was not the product of sound, impartial criticism. He attempted to reintroduce them to the world by publishing a little volume of "Readings from Crabbe," produced in the last year of his life, but without success. A different fate awaited his "Agamemnon: a tragedy taken from Æschylus," which was first printed privately by him, and afterwards published with alterations in 1876. It is a very free rendering from the Greek, and full of a poetical beauty which is but partly assignable to Æschylus. Without attaining to anything like the celebrity and admiration which have followed Omar Khayyám, the "Agamemnon" has achieved much more than a *succès d'estime*. Mr. Fitzgerald's renderings from the Greek were not confined to this one essay; he also translated the two Œdipus dramas of Sophocles, but left them unfinished in manuscript till Prof. Eliot Norton had a sight of them and urged him to complete his work. When this was done, he had them set in type, but only a very few proofs can have been struck off, as it seems that, at least in England, no more than one or two copies were sent out by the author. In a similar way he printed translations of two of Calderon's plays not included in the published "Six Dramas"—namely, "La Vida es Sueño," and "El Magico Prodigioso" (both ranking among the Spaniard's finest work); but they also were withheld from the public and all but half a dozen friends.

When his old boatman died, he abandoned his nautical exercises and gave up his yacht forever. During the last few years of his life, he divided his time between Cambridge, Crabbe's house, and his own home at Little Grange, near Woodbridge, where he received occasional visits from friends and relatives. He was one of the most modest men who have enriched English literature with poetry of distinct and permanent value, and his best epitaph is found in Tennyson's "Tiresias and other Poems," published immediately after our author's quiet exit from life, in 1883, in the seventy-fifth year of his age.

OMAR KHAYYÁM

The Astronomer-Poet of Persia

(BY EDWARD FITZGERALD)

OMAR KHAYYÁM was born at Naishápúr in Khor-
assán in the latter half of our Eleventh, and died
within the First Quarter of our Twelfth Century.
The slender story of his life is curiously twined
about that of two other very considerable Figures
in their Time and Country: one of whom tells the
Story of all Three. This was Nizám ul Mulk,
Vizyr to Alp Arslan the Son, and Malik Shah the
Grandson, of Toghrul Beg the Tartar, who had
wrested Persia from the feeble Successor of
Mahmúd the Great, and founded that Seljukian
Dynasty which finally roused Europe into the
Crusades. This Nizám ul Mulk, in his *Wasiyat*—
or *Testament*—which he wrote and left as a
Memorial for future Statesmen—relates the fol-
lowing, as quoted in the *Calcutta Review*, No. 59,
from Mirkhond's History of the Assassins.

"One of the greatest of the wise men of
Khorassán was the Imám Mowaffak of Naishápúr,
a man highly honored and reverenced,—may God
rejoice his soul: his illustrious years exceeded eighty-
five, and it was the universal belief that every boy
who read the Koran or studied the traditions in his
presence, would assuredly attain to honor and hap-
piness. For this cause did my father send me from

Tús to Naishápúr with Abd-us-samad, the doctor
of law, that I might employ myself in study and
learning under the guidance of that illustrious
teacher. Towards me he ever turned an eye of
favor and kindness, and as his pupil I felt for him
extreme affection and devotion, so that I passed
four years in his service. When I first came there,
I found two other pupils of mine own age newly
arrived, Hakim Omar Khayyám, and the ill-fated
Ben Sabbáh. Both were endowed with sharpness
of wit and the highest natural powers; and we three
formed a close friendship together. When the
Imám rose from his lectures, they used to join me,
and we repeated to each other the lessons we had
heard. Now Omar was a native of Naishápúr,
while Hasan Ben Sabbáh's father was one Ali, a
man of austere life and practice, but heretical in
his creed and doctrine. One day Hasan said to
me and to Khayyám, 'It is a universal belief that
the pupils of the Imám Mowaffak will attain to
fortune. Now, even if we *all* do not attain thereto,
without doubt one of us will; what then shall be
our mutual pledge and bond?' We answered,
'Be it what you please.' 'Well,' he said, 'let us
make a vow, that to whomsoever this fortune falls,
he shall share it equally with the rest, and reserve
no pre-eminence for himself.' 'Be it so,' we both
replied, and on those terms we mutually pledged
our words. Years rolled on, and I went from
Khorassán to Transoxiana and wandered to Ghazni
and Cabul; and when I returned, I was invested
with office, and rose to be administrator of affairs
during the Sultanate of Sultan Alp Arslan.

"He goes on to state, that years passed by, and both his old school-friends found him out, and came and claimed a share in his good fortune, according to the school-day vow. The Vizier was generous and kept his word. Hasan demanded a place in the government, which the Sultan granted at the Vizier's request; but discontented with a gradual rise, he plunged into the maze of intrigue of an oriental court, and, failing in a base attempt to supplant his benefactor, he was disgraced and fell. After many mishaps and wanderings, Hasan became the head of the Persian sect of the *Ismailians,*—a party of fanatics who had long murmured in obscurity, but rose to an evil eminence under the guidance of his strong and evil will. In A.D. 1090, he seized the castle of Alamút, in the province of Rúdbar, which lies in the mountainous tract south of the Caspian Sea; and it was from this mountain home he obtained that evil celebrity among the Crusaders as the OLD MAN OF THE MOUNTAINS, and spread terror through the Mohammedan world; and it is yet disputed whether the word *Assassin,* which they have left in the language of modern Europe as their dark memorial, is derived from the *hashish,* or opiate of hemp-leaves (the Indian *bhang*), with which they maddened themselves to the sullen pitch of oriental desperation, or from the name of the founder of the dynasty, whom we have seen in his quiet collegiate days, at Naishápúr. One of the countless victims of the Assassin's dagger was Nizám-ul-Mulk himself, the old schoolboy friend.

"Omar Khayyám also came to the Vizier to

claim his share; but not to ask for title or office. 'The greatest boon you can confer on me,' he said, 'is to let me live in a corner under the shadow of your fortune, to spread wide the advantages of Science, and pray for your long life and prosperity.' The Vizier tells us, that when he found Omar was really sincere in his refusal, he pressed him no further, but granted him a yearly pension of 1200 *mithkáls* of gold from the treasury of Naishápúr.

"At Naishápúr thus lived and died Omar Khayyám, 'busied,' adds the Vizier, 'in winning knowledge of every kind, and especially in Astronomy, wherein he attained to a very high pre-eminence. Under the Sultanate of Malik Shah, he came to Merv, and obtained great praise for his proficiency in science, and the Sultan showered favors upon him.'

"When the Malik Shah determined to reform the calendar, Omar was one of the eight learned men employed to do it; the result was the *Jaláli* era (so called from *Jalál-ud-din,* one of the King's names) —'a computation of time,' says Gibbon, 'which surpasses the Julian, and approaches the accuracy of the Gregorian style.' He is also the author of some astronomical tables, entitled Zíji-Maliksháhí," and the French have lately republished and translated an Arabic Treatise of his on Algebra.

"His Takhallus or poetical name (Khayyám) signifies a Tent-maker, and he is said to have at one time exercised that trade, perhaps before Nizám-ul-Mulk's generosity raised him to independence. Many Persian poets similarly derive their names from their occupations; thus we have

Attár, 'a druggist,' Assár, 'an oil presser,' etc.
Omar himself alludes to his name in the following
whimsical lines:—

" 'Khayyám, who stitched the tents of science,
Has fallen in grief's furnace and been suddenly
burned;
The shears of Fate have cut the tent ropes of his
life,
And the broker of Hope has sold him for nothing!'

"We have only one more anecdote to give of his
Life, and that relates to the close; it is told in the
anonymous preface which is sometimes prefixed to
his poems; it has been printed in the Persian in the
Appendix to Hyde's *Veterum Persarum Religio*,
p. 499; and D'Herbelot alludes to it in his Bibliothèque, under *Khiam*,—
"It is written in the chronicles of the ancients
that this King of the Wise, Omar Khayyám, died
at Naishápúr in the year of the Hegira, 517 (A.D.
1123); in science he was unrivaled,—the very
paragon of his age. Khwájah Nizámi of Samar-
cand, who was one of his pupils, relates the following story: 'I often used to hold conversations with
my teacher, Omar Khayyám, in a garden; and one
day he said to me, "My tomb shall be in a spot
where the north wind may scatter roses over it." I
wondered at the words he spake, but I knew that
his were no idle words. Years after, when I
chanced to revisit Naishápúr, I went to his final
resting-place, and lo! it was just outside a garden,
and trees laden with fruit stretched their boughs

over the garden wall, and dropped their flowers upon his tomb, so that the stone was hidden under them.' "

Thus far—without fear of Trespass—from the *Calcutta Review*. The writer of it, on reading in India this story of Omar's Grave, was reminded, he says, of Cicero's account of finding Archimedes' Tomb at Syracuse, buried in grass and weeds. I think Thorwaldsen desired to have roses grow over him; a wish religiously fulfilled for him to the present day, I believe. However, to return to Omar.

Though the Sultan "shower'd Favors upon him," Omar's Epicurean Audacity of Thought and Speech caused him to be regarded askance in his own Time and Country. He is said to have been especially hated and dreaded by the Súfis, whose Practise he ridiculed, and whose Faith amounts to little more than his own, when stript of the Mysticism and formal recognition of Islamism under which Omar would not hide. Their Poets, including Háfiz, who are (with the exception of Firdausi) the most considerable in Persia, borrowed largely, indeed, of Omar's material, but turning it to a mystical Use more convenient to Themselves and the People they addressed; a People quite as quick of Doubt as of Belief; as keen of Bodily Sense as of Intellectual; and delighting in a cloudy composition of both, in which they could float luxuriously between Heaven and Earth, and this World and the next, on the wings of a poetical expression, that might serve indifferently for either. Omar was too honest of Heart as well of Head

for this. Having failed (however mistakenly) of
finding any Providence but Destiny, and any
World but This, he set about making the most of
it; preferring rather to soothe the Soul through the
Senses into Acquiescence with Things as he saw
them, than to perplex it with vain disquietude after
what they *might* be. It has been seen, however,
that his Worldly Ambition was not exorbitant; and
he very likely takes a humorous or perverse pleasure in exalting the gratification of Sense above that
of the Intellect, in which he must have taken great
delight, although it failed to answer the Questions
in which he, in common with all men, was most
vitally interested.

For whatever Reason, however, Omar, as before
said, has never been popular in his own Country,
and therefore has been but scantily transmitted
abroad. The MSS. of his Poems, mutilated beyond
the average Casualties of Oriental Transcription,
are so rare in the East as scarce to have reached
Westward at all, in spite of all the acquisitions of
Arms and Science. There is no copy at the India
House, none at the Bibliothèque Nationale of
Paris. We know but one in England: No. 140 of
the Ouseley MSS. at the Bodleian, written at
Shiráz, A.D. 1460. This contains but 158 Rubáiyát. One in the Asiatic Society's Library at
Calcutta (of which we have a copy) contains
(and yet incomplete) 516, though swelled to that
by all kinds of Repetition and Corruption. So
Von Hammer speaks of *his* Copy as containing
about 200, while Dr. Sprenger catalogues the
Lucknow MSS. at double that number. The

Scribes, too, of the Oxford and Calcutta MSS. seem
to do their Work under a sort of Protest; each beginning with a Tetrastich (whether genuine or
not) taken out of its alphabetical order; the Oxford with one of Apology; the Calcutta with one
of Expostulation, supposed (says a Notice prefixed
to the MS.) to have arisen from a Dream, in which
Omar's mother asked about his future fate. It
may be rendered thus:—

"Oh Thou who burn'st in Heart for those who
         burn
In Hell, whose fires thyself shall feed in turn;
     How long be crying, 'Mercy on them, God!'
Why, who art Thou to teach, and He to learn?"

The Bodleian Quatrain pleads Pantheism by way
of Justification.

"If I myself upon a looser Creed
Have loosely strung the Jewel of Good deed,
Let this one thing for my Atonement plead:
That One for Two I never did misread."

The Reviewer to whom I owe the Particulars
of Omar's Life concludes his Review by comparing
him with Lucretius, both as to natural Temper and
Genius, and as acted upon by the Circumstances
in which he lived. Both indeed were men of subtle,
strong, and cultivated Intellect, fine Imagination,
and Hearts passionate for Truth and Justice; who
justly revolted from their Country's false Religion,
and false, or foolish, Devotion to it; but who fell
short of replacing what they subverted by such

better *Hope* as others, with no better Revelation to
guide them, had yet made a Law to themselves.
Lucretius indeed, with such material as Epicurus
furnished, satisfied himself with the theory of a
vast machine fortuitously constructed and acting
by a Law that implied no Legislator; and so com-
posing himself into a Stoical rather than Epicurean
severity of Attitude, sat down to contemplate the
mechanical Drama of the Universe which he was
part Actor in; himself and all about him (as in
his own sublime description of the Roman Thea-
tre) discolored with the lurid reflex of the Curtain
suspended between the Spectator and the Sun.
Omar, more desperate, or more careless of any so
complicated System as resulted in nothing but
hopeless Necessity, flung his own Genius and
Learning with a bitter or humorous jest into the
general Ruin which their insufficient glimpses only
served to reveal; and, pretending sensual pleasure,
as the serious purpose of Life, only *diverted* himself with speculative problems of Deity, Destiny,
Matter and Spirit, Good and Evil, and other such
questions, easier to start than to run down, and
the pursuit of which becomes a very weary sport
at last!

With regard to the present Translation. The
original Rubáiyát (as, missing an Arabic Guttural,
these *Tetrastichs* are more musically called) are in-
dependent Stanzas, consisting each of four Lines
of equal though varied Prosody; sometimes *all*
rhyming, but oftener (as here imitated) the third
line a blank. Somewhat as in the Greek Alcaic,
where the penultimate line seems to lift and sus-

pend the Wave that falls over in the last. As usual
with such kind of Oriental Verse, the Rubáiyát
follow one another according to Alphabetic Rhyme
—a strange succession of Grave and Gay. Those
here selected are strung into something of an
Eclogue, with perhaps a less than equal proportion
of the "Drink and make-merry," which (genuine
or not) recurs over-frequently in the Original.
Either way, the Result is sad enough: saddest perhaps when most ostentatiously merry: more apt to
move Sorrow than Anger toward the old Tent-
maker, who, after vainly endeavoring to unshackle
his Steps from Destiny, and to catch some au-
thentic Glimpse of To-morrow, fell back upon To-
day (which has outlasted so many To-morrows!)
as the only ground he had got to stand upon, however momentarily slipping from under his feet.

While the second Edition of this version of
Omar was preparing, Monsieur Nicolas, French
Consul at Resht, published a very careful and very
good Edition of the Text from a lithograph copy
at Teheran, comprising 464 Rubáiyát, with translation and notes of his own.

Mons. Nicolas, whose Edition has reminded me
of several things, and instructed me in others, does
not consider Omar to be the material Epicurean
that I have literally taken him for, but a Mystic,
shadowing the Deity under the figure of Wine,
Wine-bearer, etc., as Háfiz is supposed to do; in
short, a Súfi Poet like Háfiz and the rest.

I cannot see reason to alter my opinion, formed
as it was more than a dozen years ago when Omar

was first shown me by one to whom I am indebted
for all I know of Oriental, and very much of other,
literature. He admired Omar's genius so much
that he would gladly have adopted any such interpretation of his meaning as Mons. Nicolas' if
he could. That he could not, appears by his Paper
in the *Calcutta Review* already so largely quoted;
in which he argues from the Poems themselves, as
well as from what records remain of the Poet's Life.

And if more were needed to disprove Mons.
Nicolas' Theory, there is the Biographical Notice
which he himself has drawn up in direct contra-
diction to the Interpretation of the Poems given in
his Notes. (See pp. xiii-xiv of his Preface.) Indeed I hardly knew poor Omar was so far gone till
his Apologist informed me. For here we see that,
whatever were the Wine that Háfiz drank and
sang, the veritable Juice of the Grape it was which
Omar used, not only when carousing with his
friends, but (says Mons. Nicolas) in order to ex-
cite himself to that pitch of Devotion which others
reached by cries and "Hurlemens." And yet,
whenever Wine, Wine-bearer, etc., occur in the
text—which is often enough—Mons. Nicolas carefully annotates "Dieu," "La Divinité," etc.: so
carefully indeed that one is tempted to think that
he was indoctrinated by the Súfi with whom he
read the Poems. A Persian would naturally wish
to vindicate a distinguished Countryman; and a
Súfi to enrol him in his own sect, which already
comprises all the chief Poets of Persia.

What historical Authority has Mons. Nicolas to
show that Omar gave himself up "avec passion à

l'étude de la philosophie des Soufis?" (Preface,
p. xiii.) The Doctrines of Pantheism, Materialism,
Necessity, etc., were not peculiar to the Súfi; nor
to Lucretius before them; nor to Epicurus before
him; probably the very original Irreligion of
Thinking men from the first; and very likely to
be the spontaneous growth of a Philosopher living
in an Age of social and political barbarism, under
shadow of one of the Two and Seventy Religions
supposed to divide the world. Von Hammer (according to Sprenger's Oriental Catalogue) speaks
of Omar as "a Free-thinker, and *a great opponent
of Sufism;*" perhaps because, while holding much
of their Doctrine, he would not pretend to any in-
consistent severity of morals. Sir W. Ouseley has
written a note to something of the same effect on
the fly-leaf of the Bodleian MS. And in two Rubáiyát of Mons. Nicolas' own Edition Súf and Súfi
are both disparagingly named.

No doubt many of these Quatrains seem unaccountable unless mystically interpreted; but many
more as unaccountable unless literally. Were the
Wine spiritual, for instance, how wash the Body
with it when dead! Why make cups of the dead
clay to be filled with—"La Divinité"—by some
succeeding Mystic? Mons. Nicolas himself is
puzzled by some "bizarres and trop Orientals" allusions and images—"d'une sensualité quelquefois
révoltante" indeed—which "les convenances" do
not permit him to translate, but still which the
reader cannot but refer to "La Divinité." No
doubt also many of the Quatrains in the Teheran,
as in the Calcutta Copies, are spurious; such *Rubáiyát* being the common form of Epigram in

Persia. But this, at best, tells as much one way as
another; nay, the Súfi, who may be considered the
Scholar and Men of Letters in Persia, would be far
more likely than the careless Epicure to interpolate
what favors his own view of the Poet. I observe
that very few of the more mystical Quatrains are
in the Bodleian MS. which must be one of the
oldest, as dated at Shiraz, A.H. 865, A.D. 1460. And
this, I think, especially distinguishes Omar (I cannot help calling him by his—no, not Christian—
familiar name) from all other Persian Poets: That,
whereas with them the Poet is lost in his Song, the
Man in Allegory and Abstraction; we seem to have
the Man—the *Bonhomme*—Omar himself, with all
his Humors and Passions, as frankly before us as if
we were really at Table with him, after the Wine
had gone round.

I must say that I, for one, never wholly believed
in the mysticism of Háfiz. It does not appear there
was any danger in holding and singing Súfi Pantheism, so long as the Poet made his Salaam to
Mohammed at the beginning and end of his Song.
Under such conditions Jeláluddín, Jámí, Attár,
and others sang; using Wine and Beauty indeed as
Images to illustrate, not as a Mask to hide, the
Divinity they were celebrating. Perhaps some
Allegory less liable to mistake or abuse had been
better among so inflammable a People: much more
so when, as some think with Háfiz and Omar, the
abstract is not only likened to, but identified with,
the sensual Image; hazardous, if not to the Devotee
himself, yet to his weaker Brethren; and worse for
the Profane in proportion as the Devotion of the
Initiated grew warmer. And all for what? To be

tantalized with Images of sensual enjoyment
which must be renounced if one would approxi-
mate a God, who, according to the Doctrine, *is*
Sensual Matter as well as Spirit, and into whose
Universe one expects unconsciously to merge after
Death, without hope of any posthumous Beatitude
in another world to compensate for all one's self-
denial in this. Lucretius' blind Divinity certainly
merited, and probably got, as much self-sacrifice
as this of the Súfi; and the burden of Omar's Song
—if not "Let us eat"—is assuredly—"Let us drink,
for To-morrow we die!" And if Háfiz meant quite
otherwise by a similar language, he surely mis-
calculated when he devoted his Life and Genius to
so equivocal a Psalmody as, from his Day to this,
has been said and sung by any rather than Spiritual
Worshipers.

However, as there is some traditional presump-
tion, and certainly the opinion of some learned
men, in favor of Omar's being a Súfi—and even
something of a Saint—those who please may so
interpret his Wine and Cup-bearer. On the other
hand, as there is far more historical certainty of his
being a Philosopher, of scientific Insight and
Ability far beyond that of the Age and Country
he lived in; of such moderate worldly Ambition as
becomes a Philosopher, and such moderate wants
as rarely satisfy a Debauchee; other readers may be
content to believe with me that, while the Wine
Omar celebrates is simply the Juice of the Grape,
he bragged more than he drank of it, in very de-
fiance perhaps of that Spiritual Wine which left its
Votaries sunk in Hypocrisy or Disgust.

RUBÁIYÁT · OF OMAR · KHAYYÁM

THE FIRST EDITION
OF THE TRANSLATION

RUBÁIYÁT OF
OMAR KHAYYÁM

I

Awake! for Morning in the Bowl of Night
Has flung the Stone that puts the Stars
    to Flight:
  And Lo! the Hunter of the East has
    caught
The Sultán's Turret in a Noose of Light.

II

Dreaming when Dawn's Left Hand was in
    the Sky
I heard a Voice within the Tavern cry,
  "Awake, my Little ones, and fill the
    Cup
Before Life's Liquor in its Cup be dry."

III

And, as the Cock crew, those who stood
    before
The Tavern shouted—"Open then the
    Door!
  You know how little while we have to
    stay,
And, once departed, may return no more."

IV

Now the New Year reviving old Desires,
The thoughtful Soul to Solitude retires,
  Where the WHITE HAND OF MOSES on
    the Bough
Puts out, and Jesus from the Ground
    suspires.

V

Irám indeed is gone with all its Rose,
And Jamshýd's Sev'n-ring'd Cup where no
    one knows;
    But still the Vine her ancient Ruby
    yields,
And still a Garden by the Water blows.

VI

And David's Lips are lock't; but in divine
High piping Pehleví, with "Wine! Wine!
    Wine!
    Red Wine!"—the Nightingale cries to
    the Rose
That yellow Cheek of hers to incarnadine.

VII

Come, fill the Cup, and in the Fire of
    Spring
The Winter Garment of Repentance fling:
    The Bird of Time has but a little way
To fly—and Lo! the Bird is on the Wing.

VIII

And look—a thousand Blossoms with the
    Day
Woke—and a thousand scatter'd into
    Clay:
    And this first Summer Month that
    brings the Rose
Shall take Jamshýd and Kaikobád away.

IX

But come with old Khayyám, and leave
    the Lot
Of Kaikobád and Kaikhosrú forgot:
  Let Rustum lay about him as he will,
Or Hátim Tai cry Supper—heed them not.

X

With me along some Strip of Herbage
    strown
That just divides the desert from the
    sown,
  Where name of Slave and Sultán scarce
    is known,
And pity Sultán Máhmúd on his Throne.

XI

Here with a Loaf of Bread beneath the
Bough,
A Flask of Wine, a Book of Verse—and
Thou
Beside me singing in the Wilderness—
And Wilderness is Paradise enow.

XII

"How sweet is mortal Sovranty!"—think
some:
Others—"How blest the Paradise to
come!"
Ah, take the Cash in hand and waive
the Rest;
Oh, the brave Music of a *distant* Drum!

QUATRAIN XI

XIII

Look to the Rose that blows about us—
    "Lo,
Laughing," she says, "into the World I
    blow:
At once the silken Tassel of my Purse
Tear, and its Treasure on the Garden
    throw."

XIV

The Worldly Hope men set their Hearts
    upon
Turns Ashes—or it prospers; and anon,
    Like Snow upon the Desert's dusty Face
Lighting a little Hour or two—is gone.

XV

And those who husbanded the Golden
    Grain,
And those who flung it to the Winds like
    Rain,
  Alike to no such aureate Earth are turn'd
As, buried once, Men want dug up again.

XVI

Think, in this batter'd Caravanserai
Whose Doorways are alternate Night and
    Day,
  How Sultán after Sultán with his Pomp
Abode his Hour or two, and went his way.

XVII

They say the Lion and the Lizard keep
The Courts where Jamshýd gloried and
    drank deep;
  And Bahrám, that great Hunter—the
    Wild Ass
Stamps o'er his Head, and he lies fast
    asleep.

XVIII

I sometimes think that never blows so red
The Rose as where some buried Cæsar
    bled;
  That every Hyacinth the Garden wears
Dropt in its Lap from some once lovely
    Head.

XIX

And this delightful Herb whose tender
    Green
Fledges the River's Lip on which we lean—
  Ah, lean upon it lightly! for who knows
From what once lovely Lip it springs un-
    seen!

XX

Ah, my Belovéd, fill the Cup that clears
To-DAY of past Regrets and future Fears—
  To-morrow?—Why, To-morrow I may be
Myself with Yesterday's Sev'n Thousand
    Years.

XXI

Lo! some we loved, the loveliest and the
    best
That Time and Fate of all their Vintage
    prest,
    Have drunk their Cup a Round or two
    before,
And one by one crept silently to Rest.

XXII

And we, that now make merry in the Room
They left, and Summer dresses in new
    Bloom,
    Ourselves must we beneath the Couch
    of Earth
Descend, ourselves to make a Couch—for
    whom?

XXIII

Ah, make the most of what we yet may
    spend,
Before we too into the Dust descend;
  Dust into Dust, and under Dust, to lie,
Sans Wine, sans Song, sans Singer, and
    —sans End.

XXIV

Alike for those who for To-DAY prepare,
And those that after a To-MORROW stare,
  A Muezzín from the Tower of Darkness
    cries
"Fools! your Reward is neither Here nor
    There!"

QUATRAIN XXIV

XXV

Why, all the Saints and Sages who
    discuss'd
Of the Two Worlds so learnedly, are thrust
    Like foolish Prophets forth; their Words
        to Scorn
Are scatter'd, and their Mouths are stopt
    with Dust.

XXVI

Oh, come with old Khayyám, and leave
    the Wise
To talk; one thing is certain, that Life
    flies;
    One thing is certain, and the Rest is
    Lies;
The Flower that once has blown for ever
    dies.

XXVII

Myself when young did eagerly frequent
Doctor and Saint, and heard great Argu-
> ment
> About it and about: but evermore
Came out by the same Door as in I went.

XXVIII

With them the Seed of Wisdom did I sow,
And with my own hand labour'd it to grow:
> And this was all the Harvest that I
> reap'd—
"I came like Water, and like Wind I go."

XXIX

Into this Universe, and *why* not knowing,
Nor *whence*, like Water willy-nilly flowing:
　　And out of it, as Wind along the Waste,
I know not *whither*, willy-nilly blowing.

XXX

What, without asking, hither hurried
　　　whence?
And, without asking, *whither* hurried hence!
　　Another and another Cup to drown
The Memory of this Impertinence!

XXXI

Up from Earth's Centre through the
    Seventh Gate
I rose, and on the Throne of Saturn sate,
  And many Knots unravel'd by the Road;
But not the Knot of Human Death and
    Fate.

XXXII

There was a Door to which I found no
    Key:
There was a Veil past which I could not
    see:
  Some little Talk awhile of ME and THEE
There seem'd—and then no more of THEE
    and ME.

XXXIII

Then to the rolling Heav'n itself I cried,
Asking, "What Lamp had Destiny to
  guide
Her little Children stumbling in the
  Dark?"
And—"A blind Understanding!" Heav'n
  replied.

XXXIV

Then to this earthen Bowl did I adjourn
My Lip the secret Well of Life to learn:
  And Lip to Lip it murmur'd—"While
  you live
Drink!—for once dead you never shall
  return."

XXXV

I think the Vessel, that with fugitive
Articulation answer'd, once did live,
    And merry-make; and the cold Lip I
        kiss'd
How many Kisses might it take—and
        give!

XXXVI

For in the Market-place, one Dusk of Day,
I watch'd the Potter thumping his wet
    Clay:
    And with its all obliterated Tongue
It murmur'd—"Gently, Brother, gently,
        pray!"

XXXVII

Ah, fill the Cup:—what boots it to repeat
How Time is slipping underneath our
    Feet:
  Unborn To-morrow, and dead Yesterday
Why fret about them if To-day be sweet!

XXXVIII

One Moment in Annihilation's Waste,
One Moment, of the Well of Life to
    taste—
  The Stars are setting and the Caravan
Starts for the Dawn of Nothing—Oh, make
    haste!

XXXIX

How long, how long, in definite Pursuit
Of This and That endeavour and dispute?
   Better be merry with the fruitful Grape
Than sadder after none, or bitter, Fruit.

XL

You know, my Friends, how long since in
     my House
For a new Marriage I did make Carouse:
   Divorced old barren Reason from my
     Bed,
And took the Daughter of the Vine to
     Spouse.

XLI

For "Is" and "Is-not" though *with* Rule
    and Line
And "Up-and-down" *without*, I could
    define,
  I yet in all I only cared to know,
Was never deep in anything but—Wine.

XLII

And lately, by the Tavern Door agape,
Came stealing through the Dusk an Angel
    Shape
  Bearing a Vessel on his Shoulder; and
He bid me taste of it; and 'twas—the
    Grape!

XLIII

The Grape that can with Logic absolute
The Two-and-Seventy jarring Sects con-
   fute:
 The subtle Alchemist that in a Trice
Life's leaden Metal into Gold transmute.

XLIV

The mighty Mahmúd, the victorious Lord,
That all the misbelieving and black Horde
 Of Fears and Sorrows that infest the
   Soul
Scatters and slays with his enchanted
   Sword.

QUATRAIN XLII

XLV

But leave the Wise to wrangle, and with
 me
The Quarrel of the Universe let be:
 And, in some corner of the Hubbub
  coucht,
Make Game of that which makes as much
 of Thee.

XLVI

For in and out, above, about, below,
'Tis nothing but a Magic Shadow-show
 Play'd in a Box whose Candle is the
  Sun,
Round which we Phantom Figures come
 and go.

XLVII

And if the Wine you drink, the Lip you
    press,
End in the Nothing all Things end in—
    Yes—
  Then fancy while Thou art, Thou art
    but what
Thou shalt be—Nothing—Thou shalt not
    be less.

XLVIII

While the Rose blows along the River
    Brink,
With old Khayyám the Ruby Vintage drink:
  And when the Angel with his darker
    Draught
Draws up to Thee—take that, and do not
    shrink.

XLIX

'Tis all a Chequer-board of Nights and
    Days
Where Destiny with Men for Pieces plays:
    Hither and thither moves, and mates,
        and slays,
And one by one back in the Closet lays.

L

The Ball no Question makes of Ayes and
    Noes,
But Right or Left as strikes the Player
    goes;
    And He that toss'd Thee down into the
    Field,
He knows about it all—HE knows—HE
    knows!

LI

The Moving Finger writes; and, having
    writ,
Moves on: nor all thy Piety nor Wit
  Shall lure it back to cancel half a Line,
Nor all thy Tears wash out a Word of it.

LII

And that inverted Bowl we call The Sky,
Whereunder crawling coop't we live and
    die,
  Lift not thy hands to *It* for help—for It
Rolls impotently on as Thou or I.

LIII

With Earth's first Clay They did the Last
    Man's knead,
And then of the Last Harvest sow'd the
    Seed:
  Yea, the first Morning of Creation wrote
What the Last Dawn of Reckoning shall
    read.

LIV

I tell Thee this—When, starting from the
    Goal,
Over the shoulders of the flaming Foal
  Of Heav'n and Parwín and Mushtara they
    flung,
In my predestined Plot of Dust and Soul.

LV

The Vine had struck a Fibre; which about
If clings my Being—let the Súfi flout;
    Of my Base Metal may be filed a Key,
That shall unlock the Door he howls
        without.

LVI

And this I know: whether the one **True**
        Light,
Kindle to Love, or Wrath consume me
        quite,
    One glimpse of It within the Tavern
        caught
Better than in the Temple lost outright.

LVII

Oh, Thou, who didst with Pitfall and with
    Gin
Beset the Road I was to wander in,
   Thou wilt not with Predestination round
Enmesh me, and impute my Fall to Sin?

LVIII

Oh, Thou, who Man of baser Earth didst
    make,
And who with Eden didst devise the
    Snake;
  For all the Sin wherewith the Face of
    Man
Is blacken'd, Man's Forgiveness give—
    and take!

      *   *   *   *   ❀

KÚZA-NÁMA

LIX

Listen again.   One evening at the Close
Of Ramazán, ere the better Moon arose,
   In that old Potter's Shop I stood alone
With the clay Population round in Rows.

LX

And, strange to tell, among the Earthen
      Lot
Some could articulate, while others not:
   And suddenly one more impatient cried—
"Who *is* the Potter, pray, and who the
      Pot?"

LXI

Then said another—"Surely not in vain
My Substance from the common Earth
     was ta'en,
  That He who subtly wrought me into
     Shape
Should stamp me back to common Earth
     again."

LXII

Another said—"Why, ne'er a peevish Boy,
Would break the Bowl from which he
     drank in Joy;
  Shall He that *made* the Vessel in pure Love
And Fancy, in an after Rage destroy!"

LXIII

None answer'd this; but after Silence
    spake
A Vessel of a more ungainly Make:
    "They sneer at me for leaning all awry;
What! did the Hand then of the Potter
    shake?"

LXIV

Said one—"Folks of a surly Tapster tell,
And daub his Visage with the Smoke of
    Hell;
    They talk of some strict Testing of us—
    Pish!
He's a Good Fellow, and 'twill all be well."

LXV

Then said another with a long-drawn Sigh,
"My Clay with long oblivion is gone dry:
    But, fill me with the old familiar Juice,
Methinks I might recover by-and-by!"

LXVI

So while the Vessels one by one were
        speaking,
One spied the little Crescent all were
        seeking:
    And then they jogg'd each other,
        "Brother, Brother!
Hark to the Porter's Shoulder-knot a
        creaking!"

*　　*　　*　　*　　*

LXVII

Ah, with the Grape my fading Life provide,
And wash my Body whence the Life has
  died,
  And in a Windingsheet of Vine-leaf
   wrapt,
So bury me by some sweet Garden-side.

LXVIII

That ev'n my buried Ashes such a Snare
Of Perfume shall fling up into the Air,
  As not a True Believer passing by
But shall be overtaken unaware.

LXIX

Indeed the Idols I have loved so long
Have done my Credit in Men's Eye much
      wrong:
   Have drown'd my Honour in a shallow
      Cup,
And sold my Reputation for a Song.

LXX

Indeed, indeed, Repentance oft before
I swore—but was I sober when I swore?
   And then and then came Spring, and
      Rose-in-hand
My thread-bare Penitence apieces tore.

LXXI

And much as Wine has play'd the Infidel,
And robb'd me of my Robe of Honour—
    well,
  I often wonder what the Vintners buy
One half so precious as the Goods they
    sell.

LXXII

Alas, that Spring should vanish with the
    Rose!
That Youth's sweet-scented Manuscript
    should close!
  The Nightingale that in the Branches
    sang,
Ah, whence, and whither flown again, who
    knows!

Quatrain LXXII

LXXIII

Ah, Love! could thou and I with Fate
  conspire
To grasp this sorry Scheme of Things
  entire,
 Would not we shatter it to bits—and
   then
Re-mould it nearer to the Heart's Desire!

LXXIV

Ah, Moon of my Delight, who know'st no
  wane,
The Moon of Heav'n is rising once again:
 How oft hereafter rising shall she look
Through this same Garden after me—in
  vain!

LXXV

And when Thyself with shining Foot shall
    pass
Among the Guests Star-scatter'd on the
    Grass,
    And in thy joyous Errand reach the
    Spot
Where I made one—turn down an empty
    Glass!

TAMÁM SHUD

RUBÁIYÁT · OF OMAR · KHAYYÁM

THE SECOND EDITION
OF THE TRANSLATION

I

Wake! For the Sun behind yon Eastern
      height
Has chased the Session of the Stars from
      Night;
  And, to the field of Heav'n ascending,
      strikes
The Sultán's Turret with a Shaft of Light.

II

Before the phantom of False morning died,
Methought a Voice within the Tavern
      cried,
  "When all the Temple is prepared
      within,
Why lags the drowsy Worshipper out-
      side?"

III

And, as the Cock crew, those who stood
    before
The Tavern shouted—"Open then the
    Door!
  You know how little while we have to
    stay,
And, once departed, may return no more."

IV

Now the New Year reviving old Desires,
The thoughtful Soul to Solitude retires,
  Where the WHITE HAND OF MOSES on the
    Bough
Puts out, and Jesus from the Ground
    suspires.

V

Iram indeed is gone with all his Rose,
And Jamshýd's Sev'n-ring'd Cup where no
    one knows;
   But still a Ruby gushes from the Vine,
And many a Garden by the Water blows.

VI

And David's lips are lockt; but in divine
High-piping Péhleví, with "Wine! Wine!
    Wine!
   Red Wine!"—the Nightingale cries to
    the Rose
That sallow cheek of hers to incarnadine.

VII

Come, fill the Cup, and in the fire of Spring
Your Winter-garment of Repentance fling:
  The Bird of Time has but a little way
To flutter—and the Bird is on the Wing.

VIII

Whether at Naishápúr or Babylon,
Whether the Cup with sweet or bitter run,
  The Wine of Life keeps oozing drop by
    drop,
The Leaves of Life keep falling one by one.

IX

Morning a thousand Roses brings, you
    say;
Yes, but where leaves the Rose of Yester-
    day?
    And this first Summer month that brings
      the Rose
Shall take Jamshýd and Kaikobád away.

X

Well, let it take them! What have we to
    do
With Kaikobád the Great, or Kaikhosrú?
    Let Rustum cry "To Battle!" as he
      likes,
Or Hátim Tai "To Supper"—heed not you.

XI

With me along the Strip of Herbage
    strown
That just divides the desert from the sown,
    Where name of Slave and Sultán is
        forgot—
And Peace to Máhmúd on his golden
        Throne?

XII

Here with a little Bread beneath the
        Bough,
A Flask of Wine, a Book of Verse—and
        Thou
    Beside me singing in the Wilderness—
Oh, Wilderness were Paradise enow!

QUATRAIN XI

XIII

Some for the Glories of This World; and
    some
Sigh for the Prophet's Paradise to come;
  Ah, take the Cash, and let the promise
    go,
Nor heed the music of a distant Drum!

XIV

Were it not Folly, Spider-like to spin
The Thread of present Life away to win—
  What? for ourselves, who know not if
    we shall
Breathe out the very Breath we now
    breathe in!

XV

Look to the blowing Rose about us—"Lo,
Laughing," she says, "into the world I
      blow:
  At once the silken tassel of my Purse
Tear, and its Treasure on the Garden
      throw."

XVI

For those who husbanded the Golden grain,
And those who flung it to the winds like
      Rain,
  Alike to no such aureate Earth are
      turn'd
As, buried once, Men want dug up again.

XVII

The Worldly Hope men set their Hearts
upon
Turns Ashes—or it prospers; and anon,
  Like Snow upon the Desert's dusty Face,
Lighting a little hour or two—was gone.

XVIII

Think, in this batter'd Caravanserai
Whose Portals are alternate Night and
    Day,
  How Sultán after Sultán with his Pomp
Abode his destined Hour, and went his
    way.

XIX

They say the Lion and the Lizard keep
The Courts where Jamshýd gloried and
    drank deep:
  And Bahrám, that great Hunter—the
    Wild Ass
Stamps o'er his Head, but cannot break
    his Sleep.

XX

The Palace that to Heav'n his pillars
    threw,
And Kings the forehead on his threshold
    drew—
  I saw the solitary Ringdove there,
And "Coo, coo, coo," she cried; and
    "Coo, coo, coo."

Quatrain XX

XXI

Ah, my Belovéd, fill the Cup that clears
To-day of past Regret and Future Fears:
   To-morrow!—Why, To-morrow I may be
Myself with Yesterday's Sev'n thousand
     Years.

XXII

For some we loved, the loveliest and the
     best
That from his Vintage rolling Time has
     prest,
   Have drunk their Cup a Round or two
     before,
And one by one crept silently to rest.

XXIII

And we, that now make merry in the Room
They left, and Summer dresses in new
    bloom,
    Ourselves must we beneath the Couch
      of Earth
Descend—ourselves to make a Couch—
    for whom?

XXIV

I sometimes think that never blows so red
The Rose as where some buried Cæsar
    bled;
    That every Hyacinth the Garden wears
Dropt in her Lap from some once lovely
    Head.

XXV

And this delightful Herb whose living
      Green
Fledges the River's Lip on which we lean—
  Ah, lean upon it lightly! for who knows
From what once lovely Lip it springs
      unseen!

XXVI

Ah, make the most of what we yet may
      spend,
Before we too into the Dust descend;
  Dust into Dust, and under Dust, to lie,
Sans Wine, sans Song, sans Singer, and
      —sans End!

XXVII

Alike for those who for TO-DAY prepare,
And those that after some TO-MORROW
    stare,
  A Muezzín from the Tower of Darkness
    cries,
"Fools! your Reward is neither Here nor
    There."

XXVIII

Another Voice, when I am sleeping, cries,
"The Flower should open with the Morn-
    ing skies."
  And a retreating Whisper, as I wake—
"The Flower that once has blown for
    ever dies."

XXIX

Why, all the Saints and Sages who
   discuss'd
Of the Two Worlds so learnedly, are
   thrust
 Like foolish Prophets forth; their
   Words to Scorn
Are scatter'd, and their Mouths are stopt
   with Dust.

XXX

Myself when young did eagerly frequent
Doctor and Saint, and heard great
   argument
 About it and about: but evermore
Came out by the same door as in I went.

XXXI

With them the seed of Wisdom did I sow,
And with my own hand wrought to make
    it grow;
And this was all the Harvest that I
    reap'd—
"I came like Water, and like Wind I go."

XXXII

Into this Universe, and *Why* not knowing,
Nor *Whence*, like Water willy-nilly flowing;
    And out of it, as Wind along the Waste,
I know not *Whither*, willy-nilly blowing.

XXXIII

What, without asking, hither hurried
    Whence?
And, without asking, *Whither* hurried hence!
  Ah! contrite Heav'n endowed us with
    the Vine
To drug the memory of that insolence!

XXXIV

Up from Earth's Centre through the
    Seventh Gate
I rose, and on the Throne of Saturn sate;
  And many Knots unravel'd by the Road;
But not the Master-Knot of Human Fate.

XXXV

There was the Door to which I found no
    Key:
There was the Veil through which I could
    not see:
  Some little talk awhile of ME and THEE
There was—and then no more of THEE
    and ME.

XXXVI

Earth could not answer: nor the Seas
    that mourn
In flowing Purple, of their Lord forlorn;
  Nor Heaven, with those eternal Signs
    reveal'd
And hidden by the sleeve of Night and
    Morn.

XXXVII

Then of the THEE IN ME who works behind
The Veil of Universe I cried to find
  A Lamp to guide me through the Dark-
    ness; and
Something then said—"An Understanding
    blind."

XXXVIII

Then to the Lip of this poor earthen Urn
I lean'd, the Secret Well of Life to learn:
  And Lip to Lip it murmur'd—"While
    you live,
Drink!—for, once dead, you never shall
    return."

XXXIX

I think the Vessel, that with fugitive
Articulation answer'd, once did live,
    And drink; and that impassive Lip I
        kiss'd,
How many Kisses might it take—and
        give!

XL

For I remember stopping by the way
To watch a Potter thumping his wet Clay:
    And with its all-obliterated Tongue
It murmur'd—"Gently, Brother, gently,
        pray!"

XLI

For has not such a Story from of Old
Down Man's successive generations roll'd
    Of such a clod of saturated Earth
Cast by the Maker into Human mould?

XLII

And not a drop that from our Cups we
        throw
On the parcht herbage but may steal below
    To quench the fire of Anguish in some
            Eye
There hidden—far beneath, and long ago.

XLIII

As then the Tulip for her wonted sup
Of Heavenly Vintage lifts her chalice up,
   Do you, twin offspring of the soil, till
       Heav'n
To Earth invert you like an empty Cup.

XLIV

Do you, within your little hour of Grace,
The waving Cypress in your Arms enlace,
   Before the Mother back into her arms
Fold, and dissolve you in a last embrace.

QUATRAIN XLIV

XLV

And if the Cup you drink, the Lip you
    press,
End in what All begins and ends in—Yes;
  Imagine then you *are* what heretofore
You *were*—hereafter you shall not be less.

XLVI

So when at last the Angel of the drink
Of Darkness finds you by the river-brink,
  And, proffering his Cup, invites your
    Soul
Forth to your Lips to quaff it—do not
    shrink.

XLVII

And fear not lest Existence closing *your*
Account, should lose, or know the type no
   more;
 The Eternal Sákí from that Bowl has
   pour'd
Millions of Bubbles like us, and will pour.

XLVIII

When You and I behind the Veil are past,
Oh, but the long long while the World
   shall last,
 Which of our Coming and Departure
   heeds
As much as Ocean of a pebble-cast.

XLIX

One Moment in Annihilation's Waste,
One Moment, of the Well of Life to taste—
   The Stars are setting, and the Caravan
Draws to the Dawn of Nothing—Oh, make
     haste!

L

Would you that spangle of Existence
     spend
About THE SECRET—quick about it, Friend!
   A Hair, they say, divides the False and
     True—
And upon what, prithee, does Life depend?

LI

A Hair, they say, divides the False and
      True;
Yes; and a single Alif were the clue—
  Could you but find it, to the Treasure-
      house,
And peradventure to THE MASTER too;

LII

Whose secret Presence, through Creation's
      veins
Running, Quicksilver-like eludes your
      pains;
  Taking all shapes from Máh to Máhi;
      and
They change and perish all—but He
      remains;

LIII

A moment guess'd—then back behind the
    Fold
Immerst of Darkness round the Drama
    roll'd
    Which, for the Pastime of Eternity,
He does Himself contrive, enact, behold.

LIV

But if in vain, down on the stubborn floor
Of Earth, and up to Heav'n's unopening
    Door,
    You gaze To-DAY, while You are You—
        how then
To-MORROW, You when shall be You no
    more?

LV

Oh, plagued no more with Human or
      Divine,
To-morrow's tangle to itself resign,
  And lose your fingers in the tresses of
The Cypress-slender Minister of Wine.

LVI

Waste not your Hour, nor in the vain
      pursuit
Of This and That endeavour and dispute;
  Better be merry with the fruitful Grape
Than sadden after none, or bitter, Fruit.

LVII

You know, my Friends, how bravely in my
　　House
For a new Marriage I did make Carouse;
　　Divorced old barren Reason from my
　　　　Bed,
And took the Daughter of the Vine to
　　Spouse

LVIII

For "Is" and "Is-NOT" though with Rule
　　and Line,
And "UP-AND-DOWN" by Logic I define,
　　Of all that one should care to fathom, I
Was never deep in anything but—Wine.

LIX

Ah, but my Computations, People say,
Have squared the Year to human compass,
    eh?
If so, by striking from the Calendar
Unborn To-morrow, and dead Yesterday.

LX

And lately, by the Tavern Door agape,
Came shining through the Dusk an Angel
    Shape
Bearing a Vessel on his Shoulder; and
He bid me taste of it; and 'twas—the
    Grape!

LXI

The Grape that can with Logic absolute
The Two-and-Seventy jarring Sects
    confute:
The sovereign Alchemist that in a trice
Life's leaden metal into Gold transmute:

LXII

The mighty Mahmúd, Allah-breathing
    Lord,
That all the misbelieving and black Horde
  Of Fears and Sorrows that infest the
    Soul
Scatters before him with his whirlwind
    Sword.

LXIII

Why, be this Juice the growth of God,
    who dare
Blaspheme the twisted tendril as a Snare?
    A Blessing, we should use it, should we
        not?
And if a Curse—why, then, Who set it
        there?

LXIV

I must abjure the Balm of Life, I must,
Scared by some After-reckoning ta'en on
        trust,
    Or lured with Hope of some Diviner
        Drink,
When the frail Cup is crumbled into Dust!

LXV

If but the Vine and Love-abjuring Band
Are in the Prophet's Paradise to stand,
   Alack, I doubt the Prophet's Paradise
Were empty as the hollow of one's Hand.

LXVI

Oh, threats of Hell and Hopes of Paradise!
One thing at least is certain—*This* Life
       flies;
   One thing is certain and the rest is Lies;
The Flower that once is blown for ever
       dies.

LXVII

Strange, is it not? that of the myriads who
Before us pass'd the door of Darkness
    through,
  Not one returns to tell us of the Road,
Which to discover we must travel too.

LXVIII

The Revelations of Devout and Learn'd
Who rose before us, and as Prophets
    burn'd,
  Are all but Stories, which, awoke from
    Sleep
They told their fellows, and to Sleep
    return'd.

LXIX

Why, if the Soul can fling the Dust aside,
And naked on the Air of Heaven ride,
   Is't not a Shame—is't not a Shame for
      him
So long in this Clay suburb to abide!

LXX

But that is but a Tent wherein may rest
A Sultán to the realm of Death addrest;
   The Sultán rises, and the dark Ferrásh
Strikes, and prepares it for another Guest.

LXXI

I sent my Soul through the Invisible,
Some letter of that After-life to spell:
  And after many days my Soul return'd
And said, "Behold, Myself am Heav'n and
    Hell:"

LXXII

Heav'n but the Vision of fulfill'd Desire,
And Hell the Shadow of a Soul on fire,
  Cast on the Darkness into which
    Ourselves,
So late emerged from, shall so soon expire.

QUATRAIN LXXII

LXXIII ·

We are no other than a moving row
Of visionary Shapes that come and go
   Round with this Sun-illumined Lantern
      held
In Midnight by the Master of the Show;

LXXIV

Impotent Pieces of the Game He plays
Upon this Chequer-board of Nights and
   Days;
   Hither and thither moves, and checks,
      and slays,
And one by one back in the Closet lays.

LXXV

The Ball no question makes of Ayes and
Noes,
But Right or Left as strikes the Player
goes;
And He that toss'd you down into the
Field,
He knows about it all—HE knows—HE
knows!

LXXVI

The Moving Finger writes; and, having
writ,
Moves on: nor all your Piety nor Wit
Shall lure it back to cancel half a Line,
Nor all your Tears wash out a Word of it.

LXXVII

For let Philosopher and Doctor preach
Of what they will, and what they will not
    —each
  Is but one Link in an eternal Chain
That none can slip, nor break, nor over-
    reach.

LXXVIII

And that inverted Bowl we call The Sky,
Whereunder crawling coop'd we live and
    die,
  Lift not your hands to *It* for help—for It
As impotently rolls as you or I.

LXXIX

With Earth's first Clay They did the Last
Man knead,
And there of the Last Harvest sow'd the
Seed:
  And the first Morning of Creation wrote
What the Last Dawn of Reckoning shall
read.

LXXX

Yesterday, *This* Day's Madness did prepare:
To-morrow's Silence, Triumph, or Despair:
  Drink! for you know not whence you
came, nor why:
Drink! for you know not why you go, nor
where.

LXXXI

I tell you this—When, started from the
    Goal,
Over the flaming shoulders of the Foal
  Of Heav'n Parwín and Mushtarí they
    flung,
In my predestined Plot of Dust and Soul

LXXXII

The Vine had struck a fibre: which about
If clings my being—let the Dervish flout;
  Of my Base metal may be filed a Key,
That shall unlock the Door he howls
    without.

LXXXIII

And this I know: whether the one True
    Light
Kindle to Love, or Wrath-consume me
    quite,
  One Flash of It within the Tavern
    caught
Better than in the Temple lost outright.

LXXXIV

What! out of senseless Nothing to pro-
    voke
A conscious Something to resent the yoke
  Of unpermitted Pleasure, under pain
Of Everlasting Penalties, if broke!

LXXXV

What! from his helpless Creature be
      repaid
Pure Gold for what he lent us dross-allay'd
  Sue for a Debt we never did contract,
And cannot answer—Oh, the sorry trade!

LXXXVI

Nay, but, for terror of his wrathful Face,
I swear I will not call Injustice Grace;
  Not one Good Fellow of the Tavern but
Would kick so poor a Coward from the
      place.

LXXXVII

Oh, Thou, who didst with pitfall and with
gin
Beset the Road I was to wander in,
  Thou wilt not with Predestined Evil
  round
Enmesh, and then impute my Fall to Sin!

LXXXVIII

Oh, Thou, who Man of baser Earth didst
make,
And ev'n with Paradise devise the Snake:
  For all the Sin the Face of wretched
  Man
Is black with—Man's Forgiveness give—
  and take!

*   *   *   *   *

LXXXIX

As under cover of departing Day
Slunk hunger-stricken Ramazán away,
   Once more within the Potter's house
      alone
I stood, surrounded by the Shapes of Clay.

XC

And once again there gathered a scarce
      heard
Whisper among them; as it were, the
      stirr'd
Ashes of some all but extinguisht Tongue,
Which mine ear kindled into living Word.

XCI

Said one among them—"Surely not in vain,
My substance from the common Earth was
ta'en,
  That He who subtly wrought me into
  Shape
Should stamp me back to shapeless Earth
again?"

XCII

Another said—"Why, ne'er a peevish Boy
Would break the Cup from which he drank
in Joy;
  Shall He that of His own free Fancy
  made
The Vessel, in an after-rage destroy!"

XCIII

None answer'd this; but after silence
     spake
Some Vessel of a more ungainly Make;
  "They sneer at me for leaning all awry;
What! did the Hand then of the Potter
     shake?"

XCIV

Thus with the Dead as with the Living,
     What?
And *Why?* so ready, but the *Wherefor* not,
  One on a sudden peevishly exclaim'd,
"Which is the Potter, pray, and which the
     Pot?"

XCV

Said one—"Folks of a surly Master tell,
And daub his Visage with the Smoke of
    Hell;
    They talk of some sharp Trial of us—
        Pish!
He's a Good Fellow, and 'twill all be well."

XCVI

"Well," said another, "Whoso will, let try.
My Clay with long oblivion is gone dry:
    But fill me with the old familiar Juice,
Methinks I might recover by-and-by!"

XCVII

So while the Vessels one by one were
      speaking,
One spied the little Crescent all were
      seeking:
And then they jogg'd each other,
      "Brother! Brother!
Now for the Porter's shoulder-knot
      a-creaking!"

     *   *   *   *   *

XCVIII

Ah, with the Grape my fading Life provide,
And wash my Body whence the Life has
      died,
And lay me, shrouded in the living Leaf,
By some not unfrequented Garden-side.

XCIX

Whither resorting from the vernal Heat
Shall Old Acquaintance Old Acquaintance
    greet,
    Under the Branch that leans above the
      Wall
To shed his Blossom over head and feet.

C

Then ev'n my buried Ashes such a snare
Of Vintage shall fling up into the Air,
    As not a True-believer passing by
But shall be overtaken unaware.

CI

Indeed the Idols I have loved so long
Have done my credit in Men's eye much
      wrong:
  Have drown'd my Glory in a shallow Cup
And sold my Reputation for a Song.

CII

Indeed, indeed, Repentance oft before
I swore—but was I sober when I swore?
  And then and then came Spring, and
      Rose-in-hand
My thread-bare Penitence apieces tore.

CIII

And much as Wine has play'd the Infidel,
And robb'd me of my Robe of Honour—
    Well,
  I often wonder what the Vintners buy
One-half so precious as the ware they sell.

CIV

Yet Ah, that Spring should vanish with
    the Rose!
That Youth's sweet-scented manuscript
    should close!
  The Nightingale that in the branches
    sang,
Ah, whence, and whither flown again, who
    knows!

CV

Would but the Desert of the Fountain
      yield
One glimpse—if dimly, yet indeed reveal'd,
    Toward which the fainting Traveller
      might spring,
As springs the trampled herbage of the
      field!

CVI

Oh, if the World were but to re-create,
That we might catch ere closed the Book
    of Fate,
    And make The Writer on a fairer leaf
Inscribe our names, or quite obliterate!

CVII

Better, oh, better, cancel from the Scroll
Of Universe one luckless Human Soul,
    Than drop by drop enlarge the Flood
        that rolls
Hoarser with Anguish as the Ages Roll.

CVIII

Ah, Love! could you and I with Fate
        conspire
To grasp this sorry Scheme of Things
        entire,
    Would not we shatter it to bits—and
        then
Re-mould it nearer to the Heart's Desire!

CIX

But see! The rising Moon of Heav'n
    again—
Looks for us, Sweet-heart, through the
    quivering Plane:
  How oft hereafter rising will she look
Among those leaves—for one of us in vain!

CX

And when Yourself with silver Foot shall
    pass
Among the Guests Star-scatter'd on the
    Grass,
  And in your joyous errand reach the
    spot
Where I made One—turn down an empty
    Glass!

TAMÁM

CIX

But see! The rising Moon of Heav'n
      again
Looks for us, Sweet-heart, through the
      quivering Plane:
How oft hereafter rising will she look
Among those leaves—for one of us in vain!

CX

And when Yourself with silver Foot shall
      pass
Among the Guests Star-scatter'd on the
      Grass,
And in your joyous errand reach the
      spot
Where I made One—turn down an empty
      Glass!

TAMÁM

RUBÁIYÁT · OF
OMAR · KHAYYÁM

THE FIFTH EDITION
OF THE TRANSLATION

I

Wake! For the Sun, who scatter'd into
        flight
The Stars before him from the Field of Night,
    Drives Night along with them from Heav'n,
        and strikes
The Sultán's Turret with a Shaft of Light.

II

Before the phantom of False morning died,
Methought a Voice within the Tavern cried,
    "When all the Temple is prepared within,
Why nods the drowsy Worshipper outside?"

III

And, as the Cock crew, those who stood before
The Tavern shouted—"Open then the Door!
 You know how little while we have to stay,
And, once departed, may return no more."

IV

Now the New Year reviving old Desires,
The thoughtful Soul to Solitude retires,
 Where the WHITE HAND OF MOSES on the
 Bough
Puts out, and Jesus from the Ground suspires.

V

Iram indeed is gone with all his Rose,
And Jamshýd's Sev'n-ring'd Cup where no
    one knows;
  But still a Ruby kindles in the Vine,
And many a Garden by the Water blows.

VI

And David's lips are lockt; but in divine
High-piping Pehleví, with "Wine! Wine!
    Wine!
  Red Wine!"—the Nightingale cries to the
    Rose
That sallow cheek of hers t' incarnadine.

VII

Come, fill the Cup, and in the fire of Spring
Your Winter-garment of Repentance fling:
   The Bird of Time has but a little way
To flutter—and the Bird is on the Wing.

VIII

Whether at Naishápúr or Babylon,
Whether the Cup with sweet or bitter run,
   The Wine of Life keeps oozing drop by drop,
The Leaves of Life keep falling one by one.

IX

Each Morn a thousand Roses brings, you say;
Yes, but where leaves the Rose of Yesterday?
　　And this first Summer month that brings
　　　　the Rose
Shall take Jamshýd and Kaikobád away.

X

Well, let it take them! What have we to do
With Kaikobád the Great, or Kaikhosrú?
　　Let Zál and Rustum bluster as they will,
Or Hátim call to Supper—heed not you.

XI

With me along the strip of Herbage strown
That just divides the desert from the sown,
  Where name of Slave and Sultán is forgot—
And Peace to Mahmúd on his golden
          Throne!

XII

A Book of Verses underneath the Bough,
A Jug of Wine, a Loaf of Bread—and Thou
  Beside me singing in the Wilderness—
Oh, Wilderness were Paradise enow!

XIII

Some for the Glories of This World; and
    some
Sigh for the Prophet's Paradise to come;
  Ah, take the Cash, and let the Credit go,
Nor heed the rumble of a distant Drum!

XIV

Look to the blowing Rose about us—"Lo,
Laughing," she says, "into the world I blow,
  At once the silken tassel of my Purse
Tear, and its Treasure on the Garden
    throw."

XV

And those who husbanded the Golden grain,
And those who flung it to the winds like Rain,
   Alike to no such aureate Earth are turn'd
As, buried once, Men want dug up again.

XVI

The Worldly Hope men set their Hearts
       upon
Turns Ashes—or it prospers; and anon,
   Like Snow upon the Desert's dusty Face,
Lighting a little hour or two—is gone.

QUATRAIN XIV

XVII

Think, in this batter'd Caravanserai
Whose Portals are alternate Night and Day,
   How Sultán after Sultán with his Pomp
Abode his destined Hour, and went his way.

XVIII

They say the Lion and the Lizard keep
The Courts where Jamshýd gloried and drank
      deep:
   And Bahrám, that great Hunter—the Wild
      Ass
Stamps o'er his Head, but cannot break his
      Sleep.

XIX

I sometimes think that never blows so red
The Rose as where some buried Cæsar bled;
   That every Hyacinth the Garden wears
Dropt in her Lap from some once lovely
      Head

XX

And this reviving Herb whose tender Green
Fledges the River-Lip on which we lean—
   Ah, lean upon it lightly! for who knows
From what once lovely Lip it springs unseen!

XXI

Ah, my Belovéd, fill the Cup that clears
To-day of Past Regrets and Future Fears:
    To-morrow!—Why, To-morrow I may be
Myself with Yesterday's Sev'n Thousand
        Years.

XXII

For some we loved, the loveliest and the best
That from his Vintage rolling Time hath
        prest,
    Have drunk their Cup a Round or two
        before,
And one by one crept silently to rest.

XXIII

And we, that now make merry in the Room
They left, and Summer dresses in new bloom
    Ourselves must we beneath the Couch of
        Earth
Descend—ourselves to make a Couch—for
        whom?

XXIV

Ah, make the most of what we yet may
        spend,
Before we too into the Dust descend;
    Dust into Dust, and under Dust to lie
Sans Wine, sans Song, sans Singer, and—
        sans End!

XXV

Alike for those who for To-DAY prepare,
And those that after some To-MORROW stare,
  A Muezzín from the Tower of Darkness
    cries
"Fools! your Reward is neither Here nor
    There."

XXVI

Why, all the Saints and Sages who discuss'd
Of the Two Worlds so wisely—they are thrust
  Like foolish Prophets forth; their Words to
    Scorn
Are scatter'd, and their Mouths are stopt
    with Dust.

XXVII

Myself when young did eagerly frequent
Doctor and Saint, and heard great argument
    About it and about: but evermore
Came out by the same door where in I went.

XXVIII

With them the seed of Wisdom did I sow,
And with mine own hand wrought to make it
       grow;
    And this was all the Harvest that I reap'd—
"I came like Water, and like Wind I go."

XXIX

Into this Universe, and *Why* not knowing
Nor *Whence*, like Water willy-nilly flowing;
    And out of it, as Wind along the Waste,
I know not *Whither*, willy-nilly blowing.

XXX

What, without asking, hither hurried *Whence?*
And, without asking, *Whither* hurried hence!
    Oh, many a Cup of this forbidden Wine
Must drown the memory of that insolence!

XXXI

Up from Earth's Centre through the Seventh
Gate
I rose, and on the Throne of Saturn sate;
   And many a Knot unravel'd by the Road;
But not the Master-knot of Human Fate.

XXXII

There was the Door to which I found no Key;
There was the Veil through which I might not
see:
   Some little talk awhile of ME and THEE
There was—and then no more of THEE and
ME.

XXXIII

Earth could not answer; nor the Seas that
    mourn
In flowing Purple, of their Lord forlorn;
   Nor rolling Heaven, with all his Signs re-
    veal'd
And hidden by the sleeve of Night and Morn.

XXXIV

Then of the THEE in ME who works behind
The Veil, I lifted up my hands to find
   A Lamp amid the Darkness; and I heard,
As from Without—"THE ME WITHIN THEE
    BLIND!"

XXXV

Then to the lip of this poor earthen Urn
I lean'd, the Secret of my Life to learn:
  And Lip to Lip it murmur'd—"While you
    live
Drink!—for, once dead, you never shall re
  turn."

XXXVI

I think the Vessel, that with fugitive
Articulation answer'd, once did live,
  And drink; and Ah! the passive Lip I
    kiss'd,
How many Kisses might it take—and give!

XXXVII

For I remember stopping by the way
To watch a Potter thumping his wet Clay:
  And with its all-obliterated Tongue
It murmur'd—"Gently, Brother, gently,
      pray!"

XXXVIII

And has not such a Story from of Old
Down Man's successive generations roll'd
  Of such a clod of saturated Earth
Cast by the Maker into Human mould?

XXXIX

And not a drop that from our Cups we throw
For Earth to drink of, but may steal below
　　To quench the fire of Anguish in some Eye
There hidden—far beneath, and long ago.

XL

As then the Tulip for her morning sup
Of Heav'nly Vintage from the soil looks up,
　　Do you devoutly do the like, till Heav'n
To Earth invert you—like an empty Cup.

QUATRAIN XXXVII

XLI

Perplext no more with Human or Divine,
To-morrow's tangle to the winds resign,
    And lose your fingers in the tresses of
The Cypress-slender Minister of Wine.

XLII

And if the Wine you drink, the Lip you press
End in what All begins and ends in—Yes;
    Think then you are TO-DAY what YESTER-
        DAY
You were—TO-MORROW you shall not be
        less.

XLIII

So when that Angel of the darker Drink
At last shall find you by the river-brink,
    And, offering his Cup, invite your Soul
Forth to your Lips to quaff—you shall not
        shrink.

XLIV

Why, if the Soul can fling the Dust aside,
And naked on the Air of Heaven ride,
    Were't not a Shame—were't not a Shame
        for him
In this clay carcase crippled to abide?

XLV

'Tis but a Tent where takes his one day's rest
A Sultán to the realm of Death addrest;
   The Sultán rises, and the dark Ferrásh
Strikes, and prepares it for another Guest.

XLVI

And fear not lest Existence closing your
Account, and mine, should know the like no
     more;
   The Eternal Sákí from that Bowl has pour'd
Millions of Bubbles like us, and will pour.

XLVII

When You and I behind the Veil are past,
Oh, but the long, long while the World shall
last,
Which of our Coming and Departure heeds
As the Sea's self should heed a pebble-cast.

XLVIII

A Moment's Halt—a momentary taste
Of BEING from the Well amid the Waste—
And Lo!—the phantom Caravan has reach'd
The NOTHING it set out from—Oh, make
haste!

XLIX

Would you that spangle of Existence spend
About THE SECRET—quick about it, Friend!
  A Hair perhaps divides the False and
      True—
And upon what, prithee, may life depend?

L

A Hair perhaps divides the False and True;
Yes; and a single Alif were the clue—
  Could you but find it—to the Treasure-
      house,
And peradventure to THE MASTER too;

LI

Whose secret Presence, through Creation's
veins
Running Quicksilver-like eludes your pains;
  Taking all shapes from Máh to Máhi; and
They change and perish all—but He remains;

LII

A moment guess'd—then back behind the
Fold
Immerst of Darkness round the Drama
roll'd
  Which, for the Pastime of Eternity,
He doth Himself contrive, enact, behold.

LIII

But if in vain, down on the stubborn floor
Of Earth, and up to Heav'n's unopening Door,
   You gaze TO-DAY, while You are You—how
    then
To-MORROW, You when shall be You no more?

LIV

Waste not your Hour, nor in the vain pursuit
Of This and That endeavour and dispute;
   Better be jocund with the fruitful Grape
Than sadden after none, or bitter, Fruit.

LV

You know, my Friends, with what a brave
Carouse
I made a Second Marriage in my house;
Divorced old barren Reason from my Bed,
And took the Daughter of the Vine to Spouse.

LVI

For "Is" and "Is-NOT" though with Rule
and Line
And "UP-AND-DOWN" by Logic I define,
Of all that one should care to fathom, I
Was never deep in anything but—Wine.

LVII

Ah, but my Computations, People say,
Reduced the Year to better reckoning?—Nay
  'Twas only striking from the Calendar
Unborn To-morrow, and dead Yesterday.

LVIII

And lately, by the Tavern Door agape,
Came shining through the Dusk an Angel
      Shape
  Bearing a Vessel on his Shoulder; and
He bid me taste of it; and 'twas—the
      Grape!

LIX

The Grape that can with Logic absolute
The Two-and-Seventy jarring Sects confute:
   The sovereign Alchemist that in a trice
Life's leaden metal into Gold transmute:

LX

The mighty Mahmúd, Allah-breathing Lord,
That all the misbelieving and black Horde
   Of Fears and Sorrows that infest the Soul
Scatters before him with his whirlwind
      Sword.

LXI

Why, be this Juice the growth of God, who
dare
Blaspheme the twisted tendril as a Snare?
A Blessing, we should use it, should we
not?
And if a Curse—why, then, Who set it there?

LXII

I must abjure the Balm of Life, I must,
Scared by some After-reckoning ta'en on
trust,
Or lured with Hope of some Diviner Drink,
To fill the Cup—when crumbled into Dust!

LXIII

Oh, threats of Hell and Hopes of Paradise!
One thing at least is certain—*This* Life flies;
    One thing is certain and the rest is Lies;
The Flower that once has blown for ever dies

LXIV

Strange, is it not? that of the myriads who
Before us pass'd the door of Darkness
        through,
    Not one returns to tell us of the Road,
Which to discover we must travel too.

QUATRAIN XLI

LXV

The Revelations of Devout and Learn'd
Who rose before us, and as Prophets burn'd,
   Are all but Stories, which, awoke from
      Sleep,
They told their comrades, and to Sleep
      return'd.

LXVI

I sent my Soul through the Invisible,
Some letter of that After-life to spell:
   And by and by my Soul return'd to me,
And answer'd "I Myself am Heav'n and
      Hell:"

LXVII

Heav'n but the Vision of fulfill'd Desire,
And Hell the Shadow from a Soul on fire,
  Cast on the Darkness into which Ourselves,
So late emerged from, shall so soon expire.

LXVIII

We are no other than a moving row
Of Magic Shadow-shapes that come and go
  Round with the Sun-illumined Lantern held
In Midnight by the Master of the Show;

LXIX

But helpless Pieces of the Game He plays
Upon this Chequer-board of Nights and Days;
   Hither and thither moves, and checks, and
     slays,
And one by one back in the Closet lays.

LXX

The Ball no question makes of Ayes and Noes,
But Here or There as strikes the Player goes;
   And He that toss'd you down into the Field,
He knows about it all—HE knows—HE
     knows!

LXXI

The Moving Finger writes; and, having writ,
Moves on: nor all your Piety nor Wit
  Shall lure it back to cancel half a Line,
Nor all your Tears wash out a Word of it.

LXXII

And that inverted Bowl they call the Sky,
Whereunder crawling coop'd we live and die,
  Lift not your hands to *It* for help—for It
As impotently moves as you or I.

LXXIII

With Earth's first Clay They did the Last Man
    knead,
And there of the Last Harvest sow'd the Seed:
And the first Morning of Creation wrote
What the Last Dawn of Reckoning shall read

LXXIV

YESTERDAY *This* Day's Madness did prepare;
TO-MORROW's Silence, Triumph, or Despair:
    Drink! for you know not whence you came,
        nor why:
Drink! for you know not why you go, nor
    where.

LXXV

I tell you this—When, started from the Goal,
Over the flaming shoulders of the Foal
   Of Heav'n Parwín and Mushtarí they flung
In my predestined Plot of Dust and Soul

LXXVI

The Vine had struck a fibre: which about
If clings my being—let the Dervish flout;
   Of my Base metal may be filed a Key,
That shall unlock the Door he howls without.

LXXVII

And this I know: whether the one True Light
Kindle to Love, or Wrath-consume me quite,
  One Flash of It within the Tavern caught
Better than in the Temple lost outright.

LXXVIII

What! out of senseless Nothing to provoke
A conscious Something to resent the yoke
  Of unpermitted Pleasure, under pain
Of Everlasting Penalties, if broke!

LXXIX

What! from his helpless Creature be repaid
Pure Gold for what he lent him dross-
   allay'd—
 Sue for a Debt he never did contract,
And cannot answer—Oh, the sorry trade!

LXXX

Oh, Thou, who didst with pitfall and with gin
Beset the Road I was to wander in,
 Thou wilt not with Predestined Evil round
Enmesh, and then impute my Fall to Sin!

LXXXI

Oh, Thou, who Man of baser Earth didst
    make,
And ev'n with Paradist devise the Snake:
    For all the Sin wherewith the Face of
      Man
Is blacken'd—Man's forgiveness give—and
    take!

       *   *   *   *   *

LXXXII

As under cover of departing Day
Slunk hunger-stricken Ramazán away,
    Once more within the Potter's house alone
I stood, surrounded by the Shapes of Clay.

LXXXIII

Shapes of all Sorts and Sizes, great and small,
That stood along the floor and by the wall;
   And some loquacious Vessels were; and
      some
Listen'd perhaps, but never talk'd at all.

LXXXIV

Said one among them—"Surely not in vain
My substance of the common Earth was ta'en
   And to this Figure moulded, to be broke,
Or trampled back to shapeless Earth again."

LXXXV

Then said a Second—"Ne'er a peevish Boy
Would break the Bowl from which he drank
    in joy;
    And He that with his hand the Vessel made
Will surely not in after Wrath destroy."

LXXXVI

After a momentary silence spake
Some Vessel of a more ungainly Make;
    "They sneer at me for leaning all awry:
What! did the Hand then of the Potter
    shake?"

LXXXVII

Whereat some one of the loquacious Lot—
I think a Súfi pipkin—waxing hot—
   "All this of Pot and Potter—Tell me then,
Who is the Potter, pray, and who the Pot?"

LXXXVIII

"Why," said another, "Some there are who
      tell
Of one who threatens he will toss to Hell
   The luckless Pots he marr'd in making—
      Pish!
He's a Good Fellow, and 'twill all be well."

LXXXIX

"Well," murmur'd one, "Let whoso make or
    buy,
My Clay with long Oblivion is gone dry:
    But fill me with the old familiar Juice,
Methinks I might recover by and by."

XC

So while the Vessels one by one were
      speaking,
The little Moon look'd in that all were
      seeking:
    And then they jogg'd each other, "Brother!
      Brother!
Now for the Porter's shoulder-knot a-creak-
      ing!"

*   *   *   *   *

XCI

Ah, with the Grape my fading Life provide,
And wash the Body whence the Life has died,
   And lay me, shrouded in the living Leaf,
By some not unfrequented Garden-side.

XCII

That ev'n my buried Ashes such a snare
Of Vintage shall fling up into the Air
   As not a True-believer passing by
But shall be overtaken unaware.

XCIII

Indeed the Idols I have loved so long
Have done my credit in this World much
    wrong:
   Have drown'd my Glory in a shallow Cup
And sold my Reputation for a Song.

XCIV

Indeed, indeed, Repentance oft before
I swore—but was I sober when I swore?
   And then and then came Spring, and Rose-
    in-hand
My thread-bare Penitence apieces tore.

XCV

And much as Wine has play'd the Infidel,
And robb'd me of my Robe of Honour—Well,
   I wonder often what the Vintners buy
One half so precious as the stuff they sell.

XCVI

Yet Ah, that Spring should vanish with the
     Rose!
That Youth's sweet-scented manuscript
     should close!
   The Nightingale that in the branches sang,
Ah, whence, and whither flown again, who
     knows!

XCVII

Would but the Desert of the Fountain yield
One glimpse—if dimly, yet indeed, reveal'd,
To which the fainting Traveller might
spring,
As springs the trampled herbage of the field!

XCVIII

Would but some wingéd Angel ere too late
Arrest the yet unfolded Roll of Fate,
And make the stern Recorder otherwise
Enregister, or quite obliterate!

XCIX

Ah, Love! could you and I with Him conspire
To grasp this sorry Scheme of Things entire,
    Would not we shatter it to bits—and then
Re-mould it nearer to the Heart's Desire!

*   *   *   *   *

C

Yon rising Moon that looks for us again—
How oft hereafter will she wax and wane;
    How oft hereafter rising look for us
Through this same Garden—and for *one* in
        vain!

CI

And when like her, oh, Sákí, you shall pass
Among the Guests Star-scatter'd on the
    Grass,
  And in your joyous errand reach the spot
Where I made One—turn down an empty
    Glass!

TAMÁM

RUBÁIYÁT · OF OMAR · KHAYYÁM

VARIATIONS IN
THE THIRD EDITION
OF THE TRANSLATION

In the first draught of the Third Edition
the first quatrain stood thus:

Wake! For the Sun before him into Night
A signal flung that put the Stars to flight;
  And, to the field of Heav'n ascending,
      strikes
The Sultán's Turret with a Shaft of Light.

The tenth quatrain read thus in the
Third Edition:

Well, let it take them! What have we to do
With Kaikobád the Great, or Kaikhosrú?
  Let Zál and Rustum thunder as they will,
Or Hátim Tai "To supper!"—heed not you.

In the first draught of Third Edition the
thirty-eighth verse was as follows:

For, in your Ear a moment—of the same
Poor Earth from which that Human whisper
    came,
    The luckless Mould in which Mankind
        was cast
They did compose, and call'd him by the
    name.

In the final draught of the Third Edition it
was changed to read:

Listen—a moment listen!—Of the same
Poor Earth from which that Human Whisper
    came,
    The luckless Mould in which Mankind
        was cast
They did compose, and call'd him by the
    name.

In the first draught of Third Edition quatrain forty ran thus:

As then the Tulip from her wonted sup
Of Wine from Heav'n her little Tass lifts up,
    Do you, twin offspring of the soil, till
        Heav'n
To Earth invert you like an empty cup.

The first draught of the Third Edition car-
ried quatrain forty-two as follows:

And if the Cup, and if the Lip you press,
End in what All begins and ends in—Yes;
    Imagine then you *are* what heretofore
You *were*—hereafter you shall not be less.

Quatrain forty-eight in the first draught of Third Edition read:

A Moment's Halt—a momentary taste
Of BEING from the Well amid the Waste—
  Before the starting Caravan has reach'd
The Nothing it set out from—Oh, make
    haste!

In the final draught of Third Edition the same stanza ran:

A Moment's Halt—a momentary taste
Of BEING from the Well amid the Waste—
  And Lo!—the phantom Caravan has reach'd
The Nothing it set out from—Oh, make
    haste!

In the first draught of the Third Edition, there
stood the following quatrain, later deleted:

Better, oh, better, cancel from the Scroll
Of Universe one luckless Human Soul,
   Than drop by drop enlarge the Flood that
      rolls
Hoarser with Anguish as the Ages Roll.

